BASIC / NOT BORING
LANGUAGE SKILLS

WRITING

Grades 6–8[+]

Inventive Exercises to Sharpen
Skills and Raise Achievement

Series Concept & Development
by Imogene Forte & Marjorie Frank
Exercises by Joy MacKenzie

Incentive Publications, Inc.
Nashville, Tennessee

Thank you to the students who contributed works
to this book. All written material, other than that in
public domain, is used by permission.

About the cover:
Bound resist, or tie dye, is the most ancient known method
of fabric surface design. The brilliance of the basic tie dye
design on this cover reflects the possibilities that emerge
from the mastery of basic skills.

Illustrated by Kathleen Bullock
Cover art by Mary Patricia Deprez, dba Tye Dye Mary®
Cover design by Marta Drayton, Joe Shibley, and W. Paul Nance
Edited by Anna Quinn

ISBN 0-86530-365-7

2   3   4   5   6   7   8   9   10   09   08   07   06

TABLE OF CONTENTS

CELEBRATE BASIC WRITING SKILLS

Basic does not mean boring! There certainly is nothing dull about . . .
  . . . visiting with viruses
  . . . using powerful words to describe a speeding comet or an angry
      teenager
  . . . telling the difference between horrible, putrid, gritty, acrid, and
      fragrant
  . . . becoming a supersnoop for a day
  . . . enjoying sounds and rhythms of words like *schmooze, bouillabaisse,
      tessellate,* and *gadzooks*
  . . . figuring out who the victim is in a poem called "Gotcha!"
  . . . solving a brain buster for a traveling Boston businessman
  . . . creating bodacious beginnings, smashing endings, and tantalizing
      titles
  . . . straightening out mixed-up lines in stories by other kids
  . . . describing one of history's worst rogues

The idea of celebrating basic skills is just what it sounds like—enjoying
and improving the basic skills needed for writing. The pages that follow
are full of exercises and tasks that will help students review and
strengthen specific writing skills. This is not just another ordinary, "fill-
in-the-blanks" way to learn. The high-interest exercises will put kids to
work using important writing skills while they're enjoying surprising,
challenging adventures with writing tasks.

The pages in this book can be used in many ways:
  • for individual students to sharpen or practice a skill
  • with a small group needing to relearn or strengthen a skill
  • as an instructional tool for teaching a skill to any size group
  • by students working on their own
  • by students working under the direction of a teacher or parent

**Each page may be used to introduce a new skill, reinforce a skill, or
assess a student's performance of a skill.**

As students take on the challenges of these adventures with writing,
they will grow in their mastery of writing skills and will enjoy learning to
the fullest. And as you watch them check off the basic writing skills
they've strengthened, you can celebrate with them!

SKILLS CHECKLIST FOR WRITING

✔	SKILL	PAGE(S)
	Make precise word choices	10, 11
	Use effective words (specific, unusual, colorful, active, etc.)	10, 11, 12, 13, 15
	Use active rather than inactive words	13, 14
	Choose words that produce strong visual images	14
	Avoid unnecessary or repetitive words, phrases, ideas, sentences	16
	Avoid overused words, phrases, and clichés	17
	Arrange words within sentences for clarity	18
	Arrange words within sentences for interesting sound	19
	Make strong connections between ideas or parts of the piece	20
	Create sentences and paragraphs that are fluid	20, 47
	Include elements that are surprising, unusual, or extraordinary	21
	Arrange sentences for proper sequence	22
	Create strong titles	23
	Create sentences with interesting rhythm	24, 25
	Create smashing beginnings	26, 27
	Create pieces that have strong beginnings, middles, and ends	26, 28, 29, 48, 49
	Create strong endings	28, 29
	Vary sentence length and structure	30, 31
	Choose words, phrases, and style to create a certain mood	32, 33
	Use dialogue effectively	34
	Adapt form, style, or content for a specific purpose	42
	Adapt form, style, or content for a specific audience	35, 36, 37
	Include literary techniques to make writing effective	38, 39, 42
	Experiment with many different forms of writing	40, 41, 43-52
	Use writing skills to write a report	43
	Use writing skills to write a descriptive piece	44, 45
	Use writing skills to write an expository piece	46
	Use writing skills to write an imaginative narrative tale	47
	Use writing skills to write a characterization	48, 49
	Show clear organization within a written piece	43-49
	Create pieces that reveal and support the main idea well	48, 49
	Use writing skills to write on topics of personal choice	50, 51
	Infuse personal flavor (voice) into the piece	50, 51
	Use writing skills to write a persuasive piece	52

WRITING
Skills Exercises

MAKE YOUR MOVE!

Go, walk, run, jump, fly, move—these are fine English words, but they are very imprecise in that they do not describe exactly **how** a character or object relocates itself in space. Of course, the best word choice depends on who or what is moving and under what conditions.

Example: An elephant **lumbers** when he moves, while a mouse **scurries**.

For each suggestion below, choose a verb that means the same as one of the italicized words at the top of the page, but is more precise. Avoid the obvious word. Use an answer only once. Try to make a perfect match of each noun and verb! (Use your thesaurus if necessary.) Then share your answers with one of your classmates. See how many verbs you wrote that no one else chose.

hot fudge	_____	tired hikers	_____
angry teenager	_____	speeding bullet	_____
snake	_____	canary	_____
hail	_____	Olympic runner	_____
sky diver	_____	dust	_____
pole vaulter	_____	jet	_____
wild horse	_____	army tank	_____
wind	_____	kite	_____
avalanche	_____	worm	_____
snake	_____	comet	_____
broom	_____	feeble man	_____
leaf	_____	ocean storm	_____
ice skater	_____	falling dishes	_____
penguin	_____	toes	_____
brass band	_____	volcanic ash	_____
plump walrus	_____	syrup	_____
snowflakes	_____	surfboard	_____
football player	_____	sleepy toddler	_____
stream	_____		

Name _____

PRECISE IS POWERFUL

> I MET A REALLY NICE GUY WITH A GREAT PERSONALITY AND A FANTASTIC SMILE. HIS CLOTHES WERE INTERESTING AND HE HAD SOME WONDERFUL IDEAS ABOUT AWESOME PLACES TO GO ON OUTDOOR ADVENTURES.

Pretty trite words for such a find, don't you think? Hey, the reader would probably flip if this new acquaintance were described so precisely that he could be accurately pictured. Make him come alive! (You may change the gender if you wish, and use your thesaurus to find the most powerful, descriptive words possible . . . Make your reader want to meet this person!!)

I met a (an) _____ guy (girl) with a (an)_____ personality

and a (an) _____ smile. Her (his) clothes were _____

and he (she) had _____ (of) _____

ideas about _____ places to go on great adventures.

Now, captivate your reader with a description of your day with this new friend. Use only precise, powerful verbs and adjectives. Don't allow even one ordinary, overused word creep in!

Here's your opening sentence.

You'll never believe the _____ day we had!

_____

_____

_____

_____

_____

_____

_____

Name _____

SENSE-ABLE WORD CHOICES

A writer's job is to affect the reader as strongly as possible. The more sad, happy, satisfied, angry, annoyed, explosive, excited, etc. the reader's reaction to the piece, the more successful the writing!!

One effective way to evoke a strong response in a reader is to assault his or her senses with the most vivid images possible. The images may challenge any one or more of the reader's senses—touch, taste, smell, sight, or hearing. To practice making effective word choices, select the most precise word for each sentence from the parentheses in the sentences below.

PUTRID   RANCID   NOXIOUS   DISGUSTING
STOMACH-TURNING   REVOLTING   REPULSIVE   HORRIBLE   Nauseating

1. The engine (made an awful sound, hissed and sputtered its objections).
2. A (wonderful, spicy) holiday aroma filled the warm kitchen.
3. The garbage bin emitted a (horrible, putrid) odor.
4. His coat was (old and torn, worn and tattered).
5. Her fingernails on the glass (hurt, grated against) my ears.

Add at least eight additional vivid words to each list below.

TASTE	TOUCH	SMELL	SIGHT	SOUND
acrid peppery	gritty rubbery	fragrant rancid	luminous angular	murmur excruciating

On a separate sheet of paper, write a short piece that creates an extraordinary, sensory experience. You must address at least three of the five senses by using the most effective words possible to evoke reader response.

Name

IT IS WRITTEN—I WROTE IT!

The title above gives examples of both the passive and the active voice. A verb is in **active voice** when its action is **performed by** its subject. A verb is in **passive voice** when the action is **performed on** the subject.

> *Example:* **Active:** The car hit the tree.
> **Passive:** The tree was hit by the car.

Passive voice puts the action of a sentence in a weak and awkward position. Active voice usually makes writing more forceful and dynamic. (High school and college teachers often give less credit to written work which consistently employs passive voice.)

The sentences below employ either active or passive verbs. Smile when you read each active sentence. Rewrite each passive sentence to make it active.

1. The teacher taught the lesson.

   _____

2. We were embarrassed by the bad joke.

   _____

3. My purse was stolen.

   _____

4. I recognized the thief!

   _____

5. The thief was put in jail.

   _____

6. I've lost my mind!

   _____

7. Have the grades been recorded?

   _____

8. The story has never been told.

   _____

9. Are those the eggs brought by the Easter bunny?

   _____

10. Is this the hat upon which an elephant sat?

    _____

Name _____

WINDS THAT SIGH & CLOUDS THAT CRY

A favorite, easy way to begin practicing the use of strong visual images is to **personify**—give human attributes and actions to—things, ideas, and qualities.

Write a human action next to each object listed below. Then expand your description by thinking about when, where, why, or how the action might happen.

I'M REALLY BURNED UP !

Example:
- The motor coughed, choked by the bitter cold. *(why)*
- The river nestled lazily into its sandy bed. *(how) (where)*
- The rosebush slowly spread its toes in the warming mud of spring and sighed happily. *(how) (where)*

The toaster _____

The sun _____

The crowd _____

Numbers _____

The diamond _____

Our porch light _____

The traffic _____

The fog _____

A shovel _____

The angry sea _____

Skyscrapers _____

The mirror _____

A stone _____

Raindrops _____

Her raincoat _____

My fork _____

The tree _____

His boots _____

The frost _____

Candles _____

A flute _____

A hole _____

Name _____

PUT THE EXTRA IN ORDINARY

It's like eating bread, butter, and beans with milk every meal of your life. Aren't you just bored to death with the everyday, humdrum, run-of-the-mill, **ordinary**? Then kick the habit. Get rid of worn-out words like *do, give, get, go, put, make,* and *take*.

Writing comes alive when you "ditch" these old standbys and access words that draw stronger mental pictures for your reader—making an ordinary experience **extraordinary**. There is power in words. You can take any character or object and change its whole persona by substituting just one strong verb.

Try these: change only the word in italics to effect a significant difference in the character.

1. The students *walked* out of the building.

    _____ (make them appear enthusiastic)

    _____ (make them angry)

    _____ (make them seem relaxed, carefree)

    _____ (make them seem introverted, withdrawn)

2. The horse *came* out of the barn.

    _____ (make the horse appear elegant)

    _____ (make the horse appear nervous)

3. The children *ran* toward the playground.

    _____ (make the children appear out of control)

    _____ (make the children appear playful)

Name _____

SUBTRACTION ACTION

If you are a middle school student, you can probably think of several people in your experience who often overexplain things, using more words than you ever needed or wanted to hear. *Economy* is a word normally associated with money, but it is also a very important idea in communication. *Verbose* (look that up!) people appear to misunderstand something about listeners. They don't see that listeners pay more attention when the speaker or writer uses only the words really needed to relay a message clearly and forcefully. One of the most difficult things a writer has to do is to subtract words. "Extra" words are not necessarily incorrect; they just clutter and sometimes confuse the message.

Example:

Verbose - There were these two, young, frightened teenagers who were always saying how they were so afraid of dentists.

Better - The two teenagers were afraid of dentists. (Eleven words can be eliminated!)

See if you can eliminate the unnecessary words in the following sentences. (You may occasionally need to replace or reposition a word or two.)

1. It seems that the only reason that she refused his invitation to the dance was that she didn't have anything to wear._____

   _____

2. We couldn't hear the words to the song on account of the fact that the track was too loud.

   _____

3. The room was square in shape. _____

4. If students cooperate together, they can outwit the teacher. _____

   _____

5. The thing that was so bad was John's attitude. _____

   _____

6. In my opinion, I think the assignment is unfair! _____

   _____

7. He drew three round circles on his paper. _____

8. Actually, I think the bald principal is kind of cute. _____

   _____

9. Chad is a great player who really plays well. _____

10. What I would really like is a new friend. _____

11. My parents are overprotective; they watch and monitor and examine everything I do.

    _____

12. Waitress, what is today's soup du jour of the day? _____

    _____

Name _____

16

CLICHÉ: AVOID IT LIKE ~~THE PLAGUE~~
BAD BREATH

"Quick as a wink" is how fast you'd like to get your homework done. "A mind like a steel trap" is what you need to prepare for exams. "Faster than a speeding bullet" is what you hope your time will be on your next cross-country run.

These phrases do communicate because they are familiar—perhaps too familiar! They are trite, hackneyed, ordinary, overused, worn out, unoriginal, and utterly predictable. Therefore, they lose their punch. Good writers avoid them like . . . bad breath?

Use your imagination to create the strongest and most original substitutes possible as replacements for the clichés associated with these phrases.

1. Busy as _____

2. Hard as _____

3. Slow as _____

4. Smart as _____

5. Nervous as _____

6. Light as _____

7. Uncomfortable as _____

8. Funny as _____

9. Bald as _____

10. Sweet as _____

Make up some fresh, new phrases that can be substituted for these clichés.

11. Not worth the paper it's printed on _____

12. Fit to be tied _____

13. Raining cats and dogs _____

14. Feeling down in the dumps _____

15. Looked like the back side of bad weather _____

16. They don't see eye-to-eye _____

17. Head over heels in love _____

18. Together through thick and thin _____

19. Spreads like butter _____

20. Feathered his nest _____

Name _____

ESCHEW OBFUSCATION

"Sitting in the dark, the story was scary!"

The title of this activity is a tongue-in-cheek expression that means "avoid making anything difficult to understand!" It's a good motto for writers! "Sitting in the dark, the story was scary!" Have you ever seen a scary story sitting in the dark—all by itself? Poor little story! This sentence is silly, but not unusual. Careless writers cause all kinds of strange occurrences. See if you can repair the damage by rearranging each of the following sentences to more clearly show its intended meaning.

1. While cleaning the attic this morning, a mouse scared me.

   _____

2. Paddling quietly along in the canoe, the moon shone brightly.

   _____

3. I read about the bank robbers who were caught in the morning paper.

   _____

4. Having collapsed in a convulsion of laughter, the students were worried that the teacher would never regain consciousness.

   _____

5. To earn enough money for the prom, Mr. Blake gave Joey a job mowing his lawn.

   _____

6. The fans booed the football players in the stands.

   _____

7. While eating her cat food, Mom noticed that Fluffy had a burr in her paw.

   _____

8. As a child, my mother taught me many lessons.

   _____

9. There was a tiny cottage behind the junkyard that was very beautiful.

   _____

10. On the top shelf of my locker, I could not find my math book.

    _____

11. He sold ice cream sodas to the children with tiny umbrellas in them.

    _____

12. The eighth graders were punished after the fire alarm prank by the principal.

    _____

Name

A LITTLE RIDDLE THAT RHYMES
IN THE MIDDLE

Clever title, huh? It sort of rolls off your tongue! **Sound** is one element that makes language so intriguing. One way to arrange the sounds of a language for easy listening is to create short poems that are filled with words that tickle your ears.

There's nothing quite so gooey
There's nothing quite so chewy
As a brown and gooey
Brown and chewy
Piece of caramel candy.

It sticks to your teeth
Above and beneath
Thick and glue-y
Brown and chewy
Soft and gooey
Caramel candy

— *a first grade collaboration*

The trick is to stick some silly sounds together intelligently!

In the poem and in the single sentence following the poem, underline the words that are especially fun and interesting to say and hear. Then choose from the words below some that you just like and use them to create a short poem or a group of playful sentences that will be fun to read aloud. (Of course you may use your own fun-to-say words, rather than those in the list.)

Note that words that are fun to say together usually share some common sounds at the beginning, end, or middle **or** they have a pleasing rhythm when read one after the other.

Name _____

19

THE MISSING LINKS

You've probably had a conversation with someone who suddenly changed the subject. You were left wondering what planet he or she was on. It's confusing and frustrating when a conversation jumps to a new subject without any transition or connection.

Writers sometimes have a bad habit of doing the same thing. But this problem is easily resolved by learning to use a few simple expressions that link or connect ideas. Here's how it works!

Each part of a piece of writing showcases a thought or idea. To connect those thoughts and ideas to one another and make sentences flow smoothly, you need to choose from your list of "links" (words or phrases that bridge together, or connect, one idea to the next one).

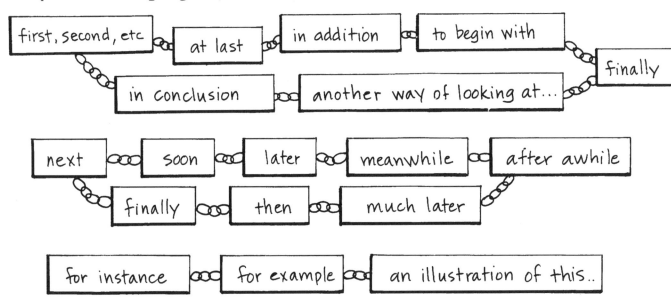

Other connecting words:

therefore	however	instead	likewise
as a result	consequently	nevertheless	similarly
accordingly	on the other hand	because of this	in spite of this

Write a composition of about 300 words in which you focus on making your thoughts flow smoothly, clearly showing your reader the relationship between each sentence or paragraph and the one that follows. Choose a topic that explains **how, why,** or **in what order** something is done. This will give you practice using your store of connecting words.

Topics:

How to memorize 100 facts for a test
Why you should never fully believe an advertisement
How **not** to fail an exam
How not to win your parents' trust and confidence
How to talk your mom into letting you have a pet boa (tiger, iguana)
A day in the life of a middle school marvel—OR, you name it . . .

Name

GOTCHA!

Up a long, rickety staircase,
Behind a creaking, rusty-hinged door
In a dark and musty attic space,
Cramped by cast-off objects, strangled by cobwebs
And obscured by decades of dust,
BLOOD
Stained a rough hewn floor where, long ago,
A murder had taken place . . .
A murder for which
The villain had never paid his debt.
An amateur sleuth
And an aspiring coroner
Could detect
Only that the blood was human,
But of the mutilated body,
Only three legs
Were left intact —
Pity!

Who is the victim in this poem? What creature would contain human blood but have more than two legs? (See page 63 for the answer.)

What fun to be caught up in a story in which the writer "sets you up" to anticipate a certain sequence of events, and then surprises you with an unusual twist or catches you off guard with an unforeseen occurrence.

Use the space on the back of this page to write a short piece that contains some surprising element. Perhaps the list below will spark an idea, but you may, of course, generate your very own!

IDEAS:

An unseen speaker

An accident

An earthquake

A storm reveals something unusual

Caught!

An explosion (of any kind)

A secret revealed

A dream that wasn't a dream

Unexpected visitor

A reversal of roles

A beginning that is an end

The shadow

A noise in the night

Flash Flood!

The trunk in the attic

The wrong person in the right place

A locked door

What's missing?

A map to an unknown place

An unusual code

A computer virus

A stampede in the circus

The lost cave

Mysterious mushroom

Name

Copyright ©1997 by Incentive Publications, Inc., Nashville, TN.

BRAINBUSTER BONANZA

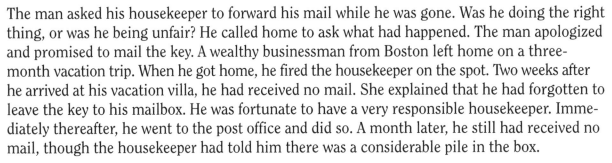

Clever Christopher could make up the best brain busters in Boston, but no one could ever solve them because the details were told in such riotous sequence as to befuddle even the most intelligent puzzle freak.

Use the space below to rewrite the clues in proper sequence. As you write, do any editing you feel will improve the flow of the piece and make it easier to read. You may even delete unnecessary words or information. Then try to guess the solution to Christopher's brainbuster.

The man asked his housekeeper to forward his mail while he was gone. Was he doing the right thing, or was he being unfair? He called home to ask what had happened. The man apologized and promised to mail the key. A wealthy businessman from Boston left home on a three-month vacation trip. When he got home, he fired the housekeeper on the spot. Two weeks after he arrived at his vacation villa, he had received no mail. She explained that he had forgotten to leave the key to his mailbox. He was fortunate to have a very responsible housekeeper. Immediately thereafter, he went to the post office and did so. A month later, he still had received no mail, though the housekeeper had told him there was a considerable pile in the box.

(Answer page 63)

_____

_____

_____

_____

_____

_____

_____

_____

Brainbuster Solution: _____

Name _____

COMIN' ON STRONG

When you are looking for something to read for enjoyment, what attracts you to a particular book or story? What is that "something special" that begs you, "Read me! Choose me!" Sometimes it's the subject, or the book cover, or an illustration. Often, it is the title. However, there are a multitude of classic stories that do not have particularly smashing titles. Some are listed below. For each title familiar to you, create what you would consider a more appealing title for that story. Then add to the list several other books you have read, and suggest a new title for each.

A story about teeny, tiny females...?

Charlotte's Web _____

The Adventures of Tom Sawyer _____

_____

Robin Hood _____

A Christmas Carol _____

Mary Poppins _____

Pocahontas _____

The Yearling _____

The Story about Ping _____

Cinderella _____

Pinocchio _____

Romeo and Juliet _____

Hamlet _____

The Cay _____

Animal Farm _____

The Three Bears _____

The Black Pearl _____

Hoops _____

The Old Man and the Sea _____

_____

Pilgrim's Progress _____

Johnny Tremain _____

The Wind in the Willows _____

_____

Sounder _____

Treasure Island _____

West Side Story _____

Your Additions: _____

_____

What is the title of your favorite book? _____

What is the best book title you can remember? _____

Name _____

MAKING WORDS SING

A. TUM TUM TUM TUM TUM TUM

B. TUM ta-ta , TUM ta-ta, TUM TUM TUM

Read these two lines aloud to yourself.
Now clap each syllable as your read; clap loudly on the tums, softly on the ta's.
Which has the most interesting rhythm?

If you chose line B, you already understand something very important about rhythm in literature. When the rhythm of a sentence is active and playful, it sweeps the reader along. It has a whole different motion than a line that just marches along to a straight beat.

Whenever you write a sentence, read it aloud to yourself so you can hear how it sounds. If it flows easily, like a song, it has good rhythm. Read these two charming poems by the same young author. Both are lovely sensory experiences. Each uses well-chosen, delightful words and ideas. Can you tell which has better rhythm—sings or flows more easily as it is read aloud?

Love is the color of lemon drops
Love smells something like cinnamon spice
Love feels like satin against your cheek
Love is a favorite song sung twice.

Friendship is rosy red
Friendship smells like cookies baking
Friendship sounds like jingle bells
Friendship is soft and comfortable.

The rhythm of the first poem flows more easily, partly because it is more playful and more regular. Its alliteration (cinnamon spice, song, & sung) and rhyme (spice & twice) also help to make it lively and fun to hear.

To practice writing words that sing, follow the instructions on the next page, page 25.

Use with page 25.

Name

MAKING WORDS SING, CONTINUED

Use with page 24.

Use this space to create some short poems of your own. Follow the model of the Love and Friendship poems on the first page, using the senses to "show" the qualities of each idea.
Practice writing sentences that have lively rhythms. See if you can make them sing!

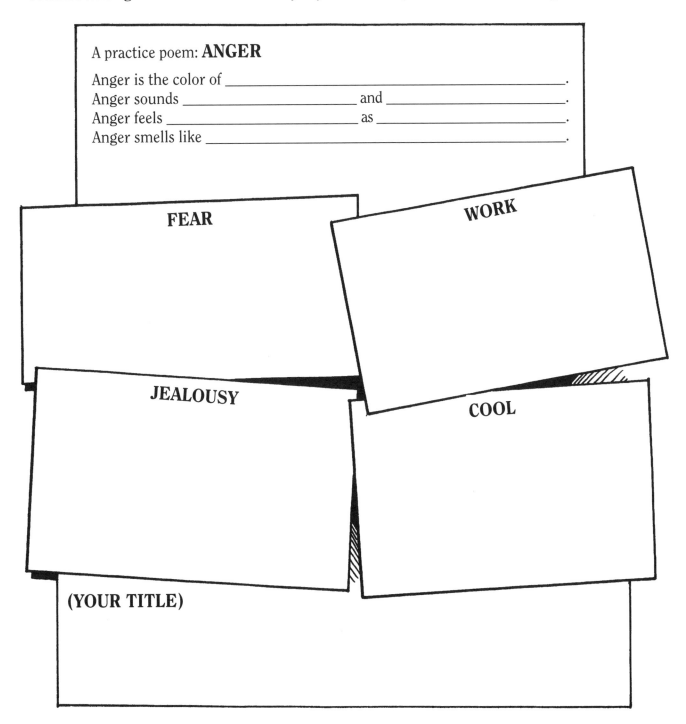

A practice poem: **ANGER**

Anger is the color of _____.
Anger sounds _____ and _____.
Anger feels _____ as _____.
Anger smells like _____.

FEAR

WORK

JEALOUSY

COOL

(YOUR TITLE)

Name _____

BODACIOUS BEGINNINGS

A. "Nothing . . . A big, hard, cold lump of nothing . . . was stuck in the pit of my stomach, and it wasn't going to go away."

OR

"Kris and I had a fight. It was one of those battles nobody wins."

BODACIOUS, MAN!

B. "Charity was a very unconventional angel."

OR

"Gadzooks!"
"Gadzooks??? What kind of language is that for an angel?"

The words you choose to begin a piece of writing are the readers' invitation to "come in." The words must be strong enough to cause the readers to believe it is worth their time to set aside whatever else they may wish to do in order to read. Writers often call these openings a "hook," because, hopefully, they hook the readers. Which of each pair of beginnings above best catches your attention and hooks you to want to read on? There is no right answer.

For at least five of the ten items below, create a smashing opening that you believe will command your readers' rapt attention. Then give each of your intended stories a compelling title.

1. the story of a storm _____

2. a warning about food poisoning _____

3. a report on safety inspections of elevators _____

4. a thriller about the capture of an international spy _____

5. a description of the best meal you ever ate _____

6. a news story of an alleged alien attack _____

7. a graduation speech _____

8. a soccer newsletter _____

9. a love letter _____

10. a memo to the school board about students' rights _____

Use with page 27.

Name _____

BODACIOUS BEGINNINGS, CONTINUED

Use with page 26.

Choose your favorite bodacious beginning. Write it on the first few lines. Then develop an intriguing body to follow your opening and close with a stunning ending. Add a compelling title.

Share your finished piece with your friends, parents, and classmates.

_____

(Title)

_____

_____

_____

_____

_____

_____

_____

_____

_____

_____

_____

_____

_____

_____

_____

_____

_____

_____

_____

_____

Name _____

HAPPILY EVER AFTER

Hutch never knew for sure whose shadow he had seen projected on the window that stormy night. But the following spring, while mulching the rose beds beneath that window, his shovel unearthed a pipe—a graceful, ebony pipe bearing a carved Egyptian symbol.

Don't you just love an ending like that—the kind that strings you along almost to the last syllable? Or do you like happily-ever-after endings?

Imaginative endings are great fun to write. With a creative ending, you can:

    . . . resolve a question, dilemma, or crisis completely

    . . . leave the reader totally hanging

    . . . leave the reader slightly mystified

    . . . teach a lesson

    . . . ask a question

    . . . thoroughly surprise the reader with a striking turn-about

    . . . use any other tactic you think will work

To write an ending, you first have to have an idea of what the piece might be about. That's where to start. Think about how to end:

. . . a report of a mysterious disappearance

. . . a vigorous protest against something you abhor

. . . a caution against a dangerous activity

. . . a wild adventure tale

. . . an unbelievable escapade into the future

. . . an apology for something you weren't all that sorry about

. . . a sad account of a disappointment or tragedy

Use with page 29.

Name

        28

HAPPILY EVER AFTER, CONTINUED

Use with page 28.

Use the empty strip spaces to create some stunning new endings. Then cut the strips apart and distribute them to a few classmates. Ask each of them to invent a good story that leads to the ending on the strip you have given him or her. Invite them to create endings for a story or stories you will write. Then find a comfortable setting in which to enjoy the stories together.

Name _____

LINE PUZZLES

Sometimes a short, abrupt sentence can make the perfect statement. On other occasions, a longer, more complex sentence best expresses what you want to say. It is difficult to write a piece that has an appealing combination of sentence length and structure. To practice this skill, work the following exercise, "Line Puzzles."

On this page and the next are four groups of short, choppy sentences. Practice your skill at "line puzzling" by combining and rearranging the sentences in the groups to form a well-composed paragraph of various sentence lengths. Be sure it will engage the reader and "flow"—read smoothly). (Feel free to change the sequence, add connecting words, etc.). Use extra paper if you run out of space here.

I have a cat.
Her name is Lacy Daisy.
That's because she is unquestionably feminine.
She also likes long, leisurely siestas.
She sips, rather than laps milk.
She tilts her head saucily.
She expects to be pampered.
She's a tease.
I love her.

Storms are scary.
They announce themselves in different ways.
Tornadoes are so sudden.
You have little time to prepare.
You can't defend yourself.
You can know too far ahead of time about a storm.
Hurricanes come slowly.
Then you have to worry longer.
You can see rainstorms boiling up in the distance.
Then they roar in on a thunderbolt.
They can come slow or fast.
However a storm arrives, I get extremely nervous.
I wish they could be stopped somehow.
I'd like to make a law against them.
I'd stamp them "Canceled!"
I would click them off like a TV.
I can't control nature.
Nature is a lot like life.
You just have to let it happen.

Use with page 31.

Name

LINE PUZZLES, CONTINUED

Use with page 30.

Saturday was a bummer.
It was raining.
The telephone rang at 6:00 A.M.
No one was up.
It was a wrong number.
Drat!
The toilet wouldn't flush.
The top had been left off the garbage.
The dog dragged the trash all over the yard.
The paper delivery service hit the window.
It cracked.
My father swore.
My mother cried.
I forgot my piano lesson was changed—to Tuesday.
I rode my bike six blocks in the rain before I remembered.
That made me miss a phone call.
It was from a girl.
She'll probably never call again.
I ate cold pizza for lunch.
I got sick.
I went back to bed.

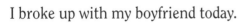

I broke up with my boyfriend today.
Well, that's not exactly true.
He broke up with me.
I didn't want this.
It wasn't my choice.
Jana told me that Brad told her.
Jesse told Brad that Mike was getting tired of me.
But Mike told Jesse not to tell anyone.
And Jesse told Brad not to tell that he told.
Brad told Jana he'd kill her if she told me.
But she did.
I asked Mike if it was true
I prayed he'd say, "No."
But he said, "Yes."
Well, he's a jerk anyway.

Name

MOOD MADNESS

Words are the tools a writer uses to "set the stage" for his or her story. The examples below illustrate how a writer sets the mood of a poem or drama in the opening lines. Notice how each author uses these lines to create an atmosphere which will influence his reader.

On the lines under each piece, see if you can identify its mood by writing a few precise words or phrases that describe the feel or atmosphere the author has created.

from *Plato's Apology*

"How you, O Athenians, have been affected by my accusers, I cannot tell; but I know that they almost make me forget who I was--so persuasively did they speak; and yet they have hardly uttered a word of truth..."

_____

_____

_____

from
"On Returning to Dwell in the Country"

"Long I have loved to stroll among the hills and marshes
And take my pleasures among the woods and fields . . ." *Tao Chien,* ancient 4th Century Chinese poet

_____

_____

from Marlowe's
The Tragical History of the Life & Death of Dr. Faustus

"Now that the gloomy shadow of the night,
Longing to view Orion's drizzling look,
Leaps from the Antarctic world into the sky
And dims the heavens with her pitchy breath,
Faustus, begin thine incantations
And try if devils will obey thy hest . . ."

_____

_____

Use with page 33.

Name _____

MOOD MADNESS, CONTINUED

Use with page 32.

Pretend you are planning to create stories on the topics below.

Write opening lines that determine the mood needed to "set the stage" for each of your new works. Just for fun, write an intriguing title for each one that is guaranteed to grab a reader's attention.

A WILD TALL TALE:

A MYSTERY:

A JUNGLE ADVENTURE STORY:

A LONG, NARRATIVE POEM ABOUT VIKINGS:

Name

Copyright ©1997 by Incentive Publications, Inc., Nashville, TN.

"HOW TERRIBLY TRAGIC," SOBBED THE READER

BINGO! This is exactly how a writer wants his or her reader to respond to a sad story. One of the saddest stories of all time is the love story of Pyramus and Thisbe. It is retold below, but the portion which appears in italics is fairly dull and awkward. Make it come alive by rewriting just this part in dialogue form. Your dialogue must be true to the story, but you should make the conversation as fascinating and suspenseful as possible. Be sure to use proper punctuation and paragraph breaks so that the story flows easily and the reader can clearly tell who is speaking. Otherwise, he or she won't be sobbing at the end! (Use a separate piece of paper.)

Long ago, there were two young lovers who lived next door to one another. Sadly, an exceedingly thick wall divided the two properties, and they were forbidden by their parents to see one another. However, as is most often the case, true love "finds a way," and the lovers talked in secret by communicating through a small chink in the great wall. One night, as the two lovers met in the shadows, they made a daring plan.

Pyramus told Thisbe that he could no longer live without the freedom to see her. Thisbe said that she was also longing to be with Pyramus—see him and talk to him without fear of being discovered. Pyramus replied that he had thought of a way that they could meet. Thisbe was anxious to hear his plan. Pyramus explained that, on the next holy day, each would get permission from his or her parents to visit the chapel in a nearby park in order to say prayers. He said that, near the chapel, was a lovely tree with thick, white blossoms. Thisbe should meet him there, just as the chapel bells struck three o'clock. Thisbe agreed excitedly. She dreamed aloud about how they would then run off together and be married and live happily ever after.

Tragically, Thisbe went to the chapel early. As she arrived, she was met by a lion in her path. Frightened, she ran to hide behind the chapel to wait for Pyramus. In her flight, she lost her veil which was picked up by the lion who had just finished a bloody dinner. As Pyramus  approached at the three o'clock bell, he observed the lion tearing at the now bloody veil. Of course, he assumed that the lion's dinner had been his precious Thisbe. Distraught with guilt that he had brought his lover to such a violent death, he took a knife from his belt and stabbed himself. As he lay dying, Thisbe peered out from her hiding place. She ran to Pyramus, but only in time to hear his last words of devotion for her. Finally united with her lover, she could not let him go alone. She took the knife from his hands and stabbed herself in the heart. The two lay together under the lovely tree whose white blossoms turned red as they drew the lovers' blood from the earth. The tree stands as a memorial to them, even to this day!

Name

ALPHABETICS

Young children are intrigued with the sounds of a language. The repetitive, playful sounds of the alphabet can become very effective tools to help them learn how to use their language. Simple rhymes such as these are joyous for them to say.

B GOES BUMP AND I CAN JUMP!

P is for punchin'
Mmmm is for munchin'
C is for crunchin'

See if you can make up an alphabet-based rhyme to go with each of the flash cards below. Decorate them, cut them apart, and try them out on your favorite kindergartner or preschooler. Then go on to the more sophisticated alphabet activity on page 36.

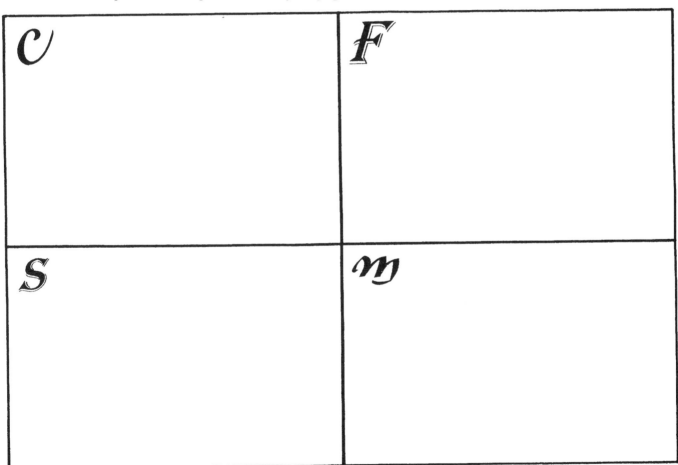

Sparkling ideas: How about . . . an animal alphabet, Christmas or other holiday alphabet, baseball or sports alphabet, music alphabet, an edible alphabet, a literary alphabet, a history alphabet . . .

Name

MORE ALPHABETICS

On page 35, you wrote some alphabet rhymes for little kids. Now change your audience focus and test your skill at a more sophisticated form of "alphabetics" by creating a poem like the one below. This poem will showcase your nomination for "Most Fascinating Letter of the English Alphabet."

Use the poem below as a model, but don't be confined by approach or form. You can write whatever kind of a poem you wish. Just make sure that it makes a **big deal** out of that letter of the alphabet. Use the space on the following page, page 37.

ALPHABETICALLY SPEAKING

B was born with a bang!
It's Bewitching
Brainy
and Beautiful!
B has a Billion in the Bank
And Believes in the Bible.
It has seen a Bazooka
in the Bayou
And a Bawdy Bartender
on a Balcony.
B Buzzes, Bops, Bites and Blabbers.
And it Beguiles,
Bedazzles and Bewilders.
It's been both a Bachelor and a Bigamist.
B is always on its Best Behavior,
Except when it Blunders
Into Bootlegging.

Marguerite & Leon, Grade 5

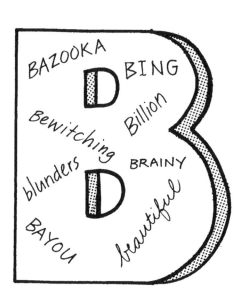

SHAN'T SURVIVE SANS SSSSSSSSS

Vote for S
It starts off some of the super-est stuff
Seven—the most perfect number
Scrumptious and sumptuous
Shush and slosh and smithereens.
You need it to snooze or sneeze or smooch.
S is great in the middle, too.
Without it you don't have kisses or wishes,
whispers or tessellations
And what a great ending! S my favorites:
mess and bless, wish and kiss (again!)
Stop and sign up for SSSSSSSSSSS!

Tamara, Grade 6

Use with page 37.

Name

36

ALPHABETICS, CONTINUED

Use with page 36.

This is a place for you to advertise one letter. Show it off. Impress everyone with how great it is. You might start by spending some time with your dictionary. Build a list of words (on a piece of scrap paper) that begin with this letter. That will give you good ideas and get you started with your poem.

I nominate the letter _____ as THE ALPHABET'S MOST FASCINATING LETTER, and here's why:

Name _____

Basic Skills/Writing 6-8+

TELL - TALE ART
(Poe - king Fun at the Famous)

Poking fun at familiar or famous writers and their writing is a sure way to get a reader's attention. If the reader agrees, he or she will cheer; if he or she is offended, he or she will grimace in disgust —either way, your writing has been effective!!

Parody (a spoof or play on words or ideas) is a favorite literary tool for poking fun. It can be used as a joke or meant to be satirical or ironic.

Example:

Silly –   (Original) "A bird in the hand is worth two in the bush."
         (Parody) "A bird in the hand is likely to soil the hand."

Serious –   (Original) "Children should be seen & not heard."
         (Parody) "Children should not be seen as a herd."

I. Try writing a parody or two, using familiar poems, rhymes or sayings as your models. Read your parodies aloud to friends or classmates and enjoy their responses!

Suggestions for a first try:

"Jack Be Nimble," "Jack & Jill," "Little Boy Blue," "Mary, Mary, Quite Contrary," "Roses Are Red," "Twinkle, Twinkle Little Star," "Time flies when you're having fun," "Don't count your chickens until they hatch" . . .

_____

_____

_____

_____

_____

_____

_____

_____

II. Now, on the next page, write a parody on a poem or piece that is a bit longer—perhaps one of your favorites from Wordsworth, Frost, Sandburg, Rossetti, Longfellow, Silverstein, Browning, or Shakespeare.

Use with page 39.

Name _____

TELL - TALE ART, CONTINUED

Use with page 38.

_____
(your title)

A parody on _____ with apologies to _____
                (title of original work)   (author)

Name

FUN WITH MULTIFARIOUS FORMS

A writer's message may be delivered to a reader in **multifarious** (look it up) forms! One simple idea can be written as a slogan, a song, a poster, a story, a chant, a speech, a letter, or a rhyme. Identify a wish or dream you have, and express your idea in as many different forms of writing as possible. On this page you will find an example idea and a variety of forms of writing you might use to express it to a reader.

IDEA— I wish I had a horse!

A PLAY

A horse! My kingdom for a horse!*

* Wm. Shakespeare's "Richard III"

A WANT AD

Wanted: Equine beast of excellent quality. Royal lineage preferred over brawn or speed. Contact I. Thackeray at Brighton Eaves, Cornwall.

A POEM

Oh, how I wish I had a horse,
A beast of elegant stature, of course –
Not the drudge of a farmer's land
Or a racer trained by a jockey's hand,
But a steed who is spirited, fearless and free,
A powerful creature of majesty!
But should my magical equine dream
Melt like a dollop of sweet ice cream
In the heat of harsh reality,
I'll have any beast of fair quality!

A TONGUE TWISTER

My speedy steed supersedes the speed of a velocipede!

Captain of the Horse Guard
Her Majesty's Royal Stables
Kensington Palace
London

31 W Brighton Eaves
Cornwall
9 October

Dear Sir,
I am writing to inquire whether you might be acquainted with a horse of elegant stature who may have proved a bit spirited for the rigorous formal duties of the horse guard and is therefore available for purchase. If so, please respond to the above address. Anxiously and humbly awaiting your kind response.

Your fellow equestrian,
Ian Thackeray

A LETTER

Use with page 41.

Name

FUN WITH MULTIFARIOUS FORMS, CONTINUED

Use with page 40.

Express a dream or wish of your own in three or four of these multifarious forms:
limerick, chant, cartoon, couplet, haiku, mystery, fantasy, recipe, me-poem,
contract, jingle, menu, news story, advertisement, résumé, announcement, ode,
bumper sticker, photo essay, song, tribute, gossip column, speech, play, banner,
conversation, or tall tale.

Name _____

INSPIRATION: IMITATION

Imitation is said to be the sincerest form of flattery. It is also an excellent vehicle for having some good fun.

A poem that Clement C. Moore wrote for his three young daughters to capture their anticipation of the Christmas Eve visit of St. Nicholas is one of the most imitated pieces in literature.
It has inspired hundreds of humorous, copycat derivatives. "The Night Before Christmas" is one of those poems that makes imitation easy and enjoyable because it is written with rhythm and rhyme that is appealing and playful. It sings! It's almost as if it has a little self-propelling motor. It "comes alive," even when read by a poor reader.

Try your skill at using at least part of Moore's poetic idea to create a new narrative tale for the purpose of explaining the anticipation of a coming event or reflecting on a past event. Choose from the several suggestions below to get your tale started—or invent your own scenario. (You don't have to make it rhyme, but imitating Moore's style and form will move it along and make it fun to hear.)

Twas the night (day, hour, moment, month, etc.) before (after)
(finals, homecoming, dinner, date nite, soccer, the hurricane, report cards) when all through the
(house, school, camp, town, etc.) . . .

'Twas the _____ before _____
_____
_____
_____
_____
_____
_____
_____
_____
_____
_____
_____
_____

'Twas the week before finals
And all through the school
Not a student was happy —
Each felt like a fool!

So they picked up their pencils
And opened their books
And started to study
With miserable looks!

Name _____

ABORT REPORT BOREDOM

The word *report* immediately sends a signal to the brain that says, "YAWN!" The dictionary definition of the word is even more of a yawn: *A detailed, formal, factual account or summation, the purpose of which is to inform.*

But a report doesn't have to be boring! If it is written well, a report can uncharacteristically make the reader's ears perk up, eyes bug out, or whole body dance. Well, okay . . . at the least, it should be written in a manner that makes the information easily readable and understandable for the reader. If it can be entertaining, that's a plus!!

Guidelines to Help You Write Dynamic Reports

1. Choose and limit your subject:
   Enough material must be available to make a report worthwhile, but not so much that you can't cover the big ideas in a few pages.
2. Locate source materials:
   Keep looking until you have found information that is fascinating to you. If you're bored, you will have difficulty making it interesting for your reader. (Don't forget that people can be resources.)
3. Take notes:
   Record only the details that are most important and have intense reader appeal.
4. Make a brief outline or plan for your report:
   An opening (including a strong thesis or topic statement) that grabs the reader's attention
   A body of riveting, reader-friendly supporting information
   A strong conclusion that makes the reader glad he read your work
5. Write a smashing, memorable account that flows easily and keeps your reader begging for more, beginning to end. You can do it!!

Suggested Topics:

How to Really Ace a Test

The Language of Dolphins

Pet Peeves of Middle School Teachers

Poisons that Lurk in Your House

Sleepwalking

How Lead Gets Inside a Pencil

Ventriloquism

Tarantulas—Tame or Terrifying?

. . . or a topic of your own choosing

Name

SENSE-SATION!

SurroundSound® is an advanced audio technique that envelopes the listener with sound from all sides. You may have heard it in a movie theater.

A powerfully written description creates the same kind of sensation for the reader; it doesn't just tell you about something, but rather, makes you see it, feel it, experience it.

Read Taylor Siegrist's description of fear. See if you agree that he has skillfully put the reader into a situation which makes him or her experience this emotion, rather than just read about it.

FEAR

The moon settles behind a thick mass of swirling clouds. You take a fleeting, desperate glance behind you and descend along the steep path into the portentously poised valley. An enormous, tangled maw of black forest gradually opens before you, and wisps of darkness clutch at your beating heart.

Phantom specters glide through the night, reaching into your soul with their scrawny, dead fingers. Ghosts dance in your mind's eye, their cold images sending chills down your spine into the core of your being. The night burgeons into a living, writhing entity which strives to strangle you in inescapable terror. The silence is interrupted only by your pulse, echoing against the valley's dark sentinels.

Thoughts of escape race in your head, then explode into hazed visages of grim torture and grizzly death. Alone, terrified, you fall to the ground, hoping for comfort in the earth's embrace. Unfortunately no solace can hide you from the pale rider in the night.

Is your heart beating a little faster than when you began reading? Perhaps you are shaking uncontrollably or your hair is standing erect on your head. If so, Taylor's piece is effective.

Choose one of the emotions listed on the next page (page 45), or identify another of your own. Use this to write a descriptive piece that causes the reader to feel that emotion intensely. Some suggestions are given to help you get started.

Use with page 45.

Name

SENSE-SATION, CONTINUED

Use with page 44.

In the space below, write a piece that describes one of these emotions (or another one you choose). Make your description powerful enough to cause the reader to FEEL the emotion, too:

joy, anxiety, loneliness, anger, anticipation, grief, surprise, longing, jealousy, disappointment, ecstasy, relief, dread, guilt, pride

_____

_____

_____

_____

_____

_____

_____

_____

_____

_____

_____

_____

_____

_____

_____

_____

_____

_____

_____

_____

_____

_____

_____

_____

Name _____

ROGUES' EXPOSÉ

Expository writing? Sounds terribly stuffy and academic, doesn't it? But look at the root of the word *expository*—*expose*. Aha! That provides a different perspective. Writing that exposes makes the unseen seen—takes its covers off and shows the reader what's underneath. Now that sounds much more intriguing!

A written piece of this sort is sometimes called—guess what—an exposé; *exposé* is defined as *an exposure of something discreditable*. (The dictionary's second meaning is much less exciting—*an exposition of facts*.)

Below is a list of some of the most famous convicted criminals, rogues, and scalawags of all times. Choose a name to research. See if you can locate a body of information about this person or group of persons that will pique the interest of readers your age. Then write an expository piece that tells the highlights of the story (What made him/her/them turn to crime? What made them so "successful?" What flaw or circumstance caused their downfall or demise?). Begin writing about your chosen rogue at the bottom of this page. Use the back of the paper for more room.

John Wilkes Booth

Sirhan Sirhan

Bruno Richard Hauptmann

Bonnie & Clyde

William & Emily Harris
(Hearst kidnapping)

Al Capone

Gotti or Gambini families

Baby-Face Nelson

Benedict Arnold

Lizzie Borden

de Medici Family

Genghis Khan

Frank and Jesse James

_____

_____

_____

_____

_____

Name

IMAGINE THAT . . .

Imagine that . . .

. . . you can't shake a shadow that is following you everywhere

. . . your best friend has just told you the world's hardest-to-keep secret

. . . something embarrassing happens as you are giving a speech before a large audience—e.g. your pants split or your skirt drops to your ankles

. . . you are nightly abducted from your room by a group of friendly aliens who return you by dawn

. . . you are chosen to sing the national anthem at a ball game, and you can't remember the words

. . . you have discovered half a wriggling worm in the hamburger from which you have just swallowed your first monstrous bite

. . . you can become invisible

. . . and so on and so on and so on . . .

Use the space below and the back of this page to create an imaginary narrative that will hold your audience at rapt attention. Your story does not have to be long, but its sentences must be dynamic and fluent. Give your readers a thrill!

_____

_____

_____

_____

_____

_____

_____

_____

_____

_____

_____

_____

Name _____

47

PERFECTION DETECTION

How would you describe each of the six characters listed below?

Under each title, make a list of qualities or attributes you associate with that kind of person. Then choose your favorite and use the outline on the following page to plan a characterization (description of that person's character). Do not merely repeat the words and phrases you have listed. Create precise word pictures that will show the reader that person's character through his or her speech and behavior.

> *Example:*
> **NOT** — Ben makes an ideal friend because he is unselfish.
> **RATHER** — "What would you like to do?" Ben always asks me, before he expresses his preference. He once loaned me his car to go to a job interview while he walked to the store in the rain to buy groceries for his mother.

An ideal friend

An absolute bore

An honor student

A high school hero/heroine

A lovable pest

A memorable teacher/coach

Use with page 49.

Name _____

PERFECTION DETECTION, continued

Use with page 48.

A PLAN FOR WRITING A CHARACTERIZATION

I. A captivating title to command the reader's attention:

_____

II. A masterful opening statement that will invite the reader to want to know my person:

_____

_____

III. Several follow-up sentences that introduce the major character traits I see in this person:

_____

_____

_____

_____

_____

_____

IV. A very strong body (one or more paragraphs) that will include these examples of behavior to support statements made in my opening paragraph:

_____

_____

_____

_____

_____

_____

V. Ideas I will use in a concluding paragraph that will summarize the character I have presented and make my reader glad to have read this piece:

_____

_____

_____

_____

_____

_____

_____

_____

Name

SUPERSNOOP

Your mission, supersnoop, is to choose a fictional or real character about whom information will be easy to track down. Pose as this person and create a journal of 8–10 entries, chronicling experiences, events, thoughts, and ideas related to his or her life. Use the space provided on the next page (page 51).

The entries may be sequential (dated in chronological order) or random. When a reader has read all the entries, he or she should be able to identify the "owner" of the journal.

This can be a challenging and entertaining activity—especially if you do your job as a "supersnoop," finding interesting and juicy information to include in your journal! Everything you write must be true to the reputation and personality of the character you are impersonating. You may have to do a bit of research to get the "good stuff!"

Remember that a journal may include all kinds of written material: very personal entries; thoughts and opinions on people and things; mini-essays related to politics, philosophy, social issues, literature, religion, moral issues, etc.; poetry; drawings or sketches; lists; notes or reminders to oneself, etc.

You can be anyone from Cruella DeVil to Winston Churchill, Mother Theresa, Hamlet, Michael Jordan, Chelsea Clinton, your English teacher, or the Pope. However, it is very important that you write in the voice and style you think that person would use—see and say things as you believe he or she would see and say them. (Of course, be sure that what he or she says is fascinating to read!)

Note: Trade journals with a friend and try to guess each other's identity.

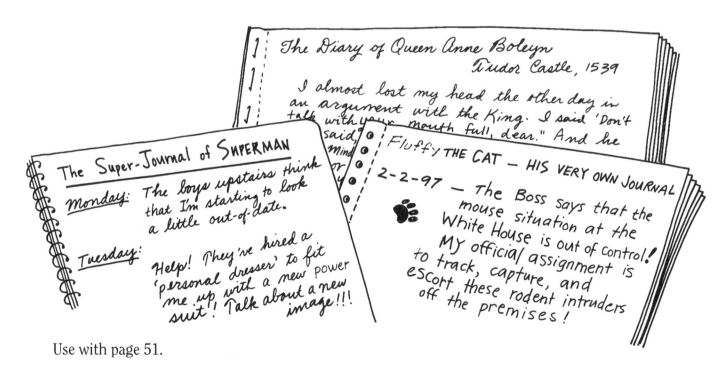

Use with page 51.

Name

SUPERSNOOP, CONTINUED

Use with page 50.

Name

51

QUOTATION QUANDARY

"A little knowledge is a dangerous thing." Really?

"The only thing we have to fear is fear itself." Do you agree?

"Early to bed, early to rise, makes a man healthy, wealthy, and wise." Is this true?

Have you ever wondered how time-honored quotations like these have come to be famous—and generally accepted as truth? Some were originally the words of famous people, but that is not necessarily what made them endure through the generations of time.

Quotations like these grow out of the discernment, enlightenment, and good horse sense offered by people of all eras of history, all culture, all ages, and all levels of education. Together they have become a kind of folk wisdom that offers guidance for everyday life. They keep finding their way into commonplace conversation, and we take them for granted—often giving little thought to their meaning. But should we believe them? Do they represent truth? What do you think?

Write a short, informal essay that takes a position of agreement or disagreement with one of the above quotations. Use a combination of your finest writing and persuasive skills to convince the reader to "buy" your bias or point of view!

BIFF'S USED CARS

WOW, DO I HAVE A DEAL FOR YOU

_____

_____

_____

_____

_____

_____

_____

_____

_____

_____

_____

_____

_____

_____

_____

Name _____

52

APPENDIX

CONTENTS

THE WRITING PROCESS

Stage 1 — The Motivation
>. . . a group experience
>. . . an individual experience
>. . . a piece of literature
>. . . an unexpected happening
>. . . a common feeling
>. . . a question
>. . . a memory
>. . . a discussion
>. . . a surprise happening
>. . . an activity in any content area

The motivation is something that sparks the writing. You provide the situation or make use of a natural one to evoke ideas, impressions, emotions, opinions, questions, beliefs, explorations, or mysteries—to bring to the surface those possibilities and imaginings which are tucked away in minds.

Stage 2 — Collecting Impressions
>. . . the gathering of words and fragments and thoughts and facts and phrases and questions and observations . . . the process of brainstorming about and broadening the original idea . . .

Stage 3 — Organizing
>. . . the time for taking a close look at all those impressions you have collected and thinking about what fits together . . . this is the time for asking yourself questions such as . . .

>>What goes with this idea?
>>Which ideas should be grouped together?
>>Where would this fit into the whole picture?
>>What do these ideas or phrases have in common?

>. . . and then using some method to visually connect impressions together. Your organizational tool may be a chart, or a web, or a storyboard, or an outline, or a series of boxes, or a diagram, or a list, or series of note cards. It can be anything that groups your usable ideas together in a way that will help you go on to connect them in your writing.

Stage 4 — The Rough Draft
>. . . the put-it-together phase . . .

This is the stage at which you say, "Okay, you've got thoughts and groups of ideas and phrases. You've thought about which of these may fit together. Now . . . write!" Start putting those words together into phrases, those phrases together into lines or sentences, those sentences together into paragraphs.

Basic Skills/Writing 6-8+

Stage 5 — Author's Review

 . . . the author's chance to get the writing out into the light and see how it looks and hear how it sounds.

 . . . This is the time for writers to ask themselves questions such as, "Does it make sense?" "Does it say what I intended?" "Do I like it?" "Is it smooth and clear?" "Are the ideas in the right order?" "Are any words or pieces missing?" and other such questions that good teachers can help kids learn to ask.

Stage 6 — Sharing for Response

 . . . a time for trading pieces, or reading to a small group, or sharing with the teacher—for the purpose of getting reactions, questions, suggestions, praises, affirmation of strengths, and ideas for changes . . .

Stage 7 — Editing and Revising

 . . . the changing, fixing stage . . . including anything from reshuffling or replacing words to reworking whole pieces

 . . . After the writer has reviewed his or her own work and gained the responses of others, then he or she is ready to make adjustments.

Stage 8 — The Mechanics Check

 . . . the time to inspect the original draft for spelling, grammar, mechanical, and structural errors or weaknesses . . .

This may be the point at which the teacher takes papers home to note (preferably with some means other than a red pencil, please) errors in mechanics (or conventions) OR looks over shoulders to point them out. A good deal of this can also be done in student groups or with the help of peers, older students, or volunteer adults.

Stage 9 — The Final Copy

 . . . the preparation of the final draft—making use of the input of all your own and others' responses on content and techniques and mechanics . . . AND the resulting satisfaction and surprise that comes with the polishing of a product . . .

Stage 10 — Presenting

 . . . the sharing, showing-off, or publishing part . . . the chance to use your written words to communicate to other persons. In some way, every finished piece should be made public if the author chooses . . .

AN EDITOR'S CHECKLIST

_____ Did you accomplish your purpose?

_____ Did you write for the audience you intended?

_____ Did you write in a way that will cause the readers to react the way you wanted?

_____ Have you clearly made your main point?

_____ Have you given clear details and examples of your main point?

_____ Do you have a variety of sentence lengths and structures?

_____ Are your sentences or lines in a sequence that makes sense?

_____ Are your sentences and ideas held together by effective, interesting connections?

_____ Does each paragraph contain sentences that follow the same idea?

_____ Do you have any sentences that say the same thing as other sentences?

_____ Do you have too many sentences that start the same way?

_____ Read your piece aloud. Do the sentences flow well? Does the rhythm sound pleasing?

_____ Do you have an interesting, reader-catching beginning?

_____ Does the middle of the piece accomplish what you want?

_____ Do you have a strong ending?

_____ Have you chosen a variety of interesting words?

_____ Have you gotten rid of repetitive words?

_____ Have you gotten rid of clichés and overused words?

_____ Have you used the most specific, colorful, and effective words you know?

_____ Is the style interesting and smooth?

_____ Have you set the tone you want?

_____ Does the piece have power, or passion, or conviction that will "draw in" the reader?

_____ Did you proofread for:

      _____ Spelling?

      _____ Punctuation?

      _____ Capitalization?

      _____ Incomplete or run-on sentences?

      _____ Agreement of verb tenses?

      _____ Words forgotten or skipped or out of order?

GOOD! Then your writing is ready to show off!

THE P-Q-P PLAN FOR RESPONDING TO WRITING AND REVISING

Here's an easy-to-use plan to guide you through the response and revision stages. The first P and the Q are response tactics: Praise and Question. The last P is the revision tactic: Polish. Writers of all ages can make improvements in their writing by remembering these three steps:

PRAISE. Writers tell each other . . . what's strong . . . what's good . . . what's effective . . . what works . . . what caught your ear or eye . . . what's pleasing . . . what sparked a thought . . . what taught you something . . . what surprised or delighted you . . . etc.

Crash! was a great choice for the opening sentence! It grabbed my attention right away.

It was a good idea to string all those short words together in this part. It made the girl seem very much in a hurry.

*I liked the way you repeated the **T** sound over and over in this poem. That gave a marching rhythm to the poem.*

*I like the wet words for your rain poem. My favorites were **slosh . . . slurpy . . . slush . . . drizzle . . . slop . . . and splatter.***

The ending was a great surprise. It really caught me off guard.

The part about the alligator swallowing the umbrella was my favorite!

I like the part about the squirmy, squishy, soft, and mushy worm.

Tom, your title, "The Food No Kid Should Eat," made me want to listen to your paragraph.

It was such a good idea to end the argument with a question. That really made me question the safety of skateboards, too.

These two sentences right here really show your sense of humor.

I like the way you started the argument by telling all the good things about fast foods before you switched to your pitch against them. That gave an unusual twist and caught my attention.

QUESTION. Writers ask questions that will help the author review and think about the writing to . . . realize where things may not be clear . . . hear where something is missing . . . notice where something could be stronger, funnier, more suspenseful, more informative . . . etc. . . . and consider what could be changed or added or removed. This is not harsh criticism. No outside opinion is forced on the writer. That's the reason for using the question form. A question is stated and left for the author to answer and decide.

Your autobiography didn't tell much about your preschool years. Could you add a few sentences about that?

How did your puppy get lost anyway?

I felt as if you gave away the ending too soon. Could you add something right here to prolong the suspense a bit?

*Could you replace the word **neat** with a different word in two of the three places you used it?*

What would you have said to this reporter? What is your opinion about this topic? I'd like to get more of a feel for your voice.

I'm confused about how the girls got into the volcano in the first place. Could you add a sentence or two to make it clear?

What color was your kitten? Was it little? How did you feel about finding her after a whole week?

Didn't the gorilla have to escape from the zoo before he sat on the mayor? Shouldn't this sentence come before this one?

What is your feeling about this earthquake? I don't get much of an idea of the author's involvement in this.

POLISH. After gaining some responses from others, the author decides what input to use . . . what suggestions to discard or include . . . what changes to make . . . which feedback is important. And then the author adds this information to his or her own ideas to put to use in a new draft. It's unlikely that all of the responses can be used. Nor should they be. That, finally, is up to the author to decide.

57

WRITING
SKILLS TEST

PART I

For items 1–5, choose the word that is the most precise one for the sentence. Each question is worth 1 point.

1. Three cold, wet six-year-olds _____ along home, wearily pulling their sleds after a long day of sledding in the woods.
   a. scampered
   b. slithered
   c. trudged
   d. ambled

2. With cheeks full of crumbs from our pantry, the _____ mouse scuttled behind the stove.
   a. plump
   b. chunky
   c. stout
   d. burly

3. Her friends were _____ by Sara's terrifying tale of falling into the sewer.
   a. provoked
   b. captivated
   c. attracted
   d. inspired

4. "Absolutely not!" _____ Mother when we told her we were going to shave the cat.
   a. shrieked
   b. drawled
   c. muttered
   d. advised

5. I wasn't prepared at all for the science test, so I went into the classroom feeling pretty _____ .
   a. alarmed
   b. shy
   c. haunted
   d. apprehensive

6–9. Choose the word or phrase that is most effective for the sentence. Each question is worth 1 point.

6. The principal gave the students a(n) _____ after she discovered the band uniforms flying from the flag pole.
   a. oration
   b. admonishment
   c. talk
   d. speech

7. Tom _____ his friend after the game and went off with some girls he'd just met.
   a. released
   b. left
   c. abandoned
   d. walked away from

8. We started a campaign to _____ drugs in our school.
   a. drop
   b. dismiss
   c. omit
   d. abolish

9. Tamara looked _____ in her black velvet prom dress.
   a. nice
   b. exquisite
   c. pretty
   d. beautiful

Name _____

Basic Skills/Writing 6-8+

For items 10–20, there may be more than one answer on some questions. Write all correct answers.

10. Which example (examples) has (have) active voice? _____
    a. Her heart was broken.
    b. She had a broken heart.
    c. Her boyfriend broke her heart.

11. Which example (examples) has (have) active voice? _____
    a. The alligator grabbed my foot.
    b. My foot is in the alligator's mouth.
    c. I put my foot in the alligator's mouth (by mistake).

12. Which example (examples) has (have) active voice? _____
    a. Who dropped the bag of jelly beans?
    b. Why are the jelly beans rolling down the hall toward the science lab?
    c. Is it true that the jelly beans are all over the school?

13. Which sentence(s) contain(s) personification?
    _____
    a. The damp fog reached its fingers into my coat.
    b. Summer has snuck up on us so quickly.
    c. Samantha is singing in her sleep.

14. Which sentence(s) contain(s) a metaphor?
    _____
    a. Lightning cracks with popcorn quickness.
    b. Jessica's popcorn is saturated with salt.
    c. This popcorn is as old as the Constitution.

15. Which sentence contains a simile?
    _____
    a. My popcorn tastes like sawdust.
    b. The hissing popcorn maker is calling us to the kitchen.
    c. Popcorn is expensive at the movie theater.

16. Which words are unnecessary in this sentence?

    _____
    _____
    _____
    _____

    This old man who was kind of like older than my grandpa went skydiving together with my brother.

17. Which sentence(s) contain(s) alliteration?
    _____
    a. Don't you dare drop doughnuts down the downstairs drain.
    b. Grimy, slimy, wiggly, squiggly things are coming out of my salad.
    c. Crash! Bang! Slam! What is going on down there?

18. Which sentence(s) do(es) NOT include a metaphor? _____
    a. My English teacher is as sour as a lemon today.
    b. The numbers on my clock glow eerily green in the dark night.
    c. My hair grows faster than you do your homework.

19. Which sentence(s) evoke(s) a strong visual image? _____
    a. Traffic lights make me wildly impatient.
    b. The traffic light winked its yellow eye at me.
    c. This traffic light has the longest yellow in the city.

20. Which sentence(s) do(es) NOT evoke a strong visual image? _____
    a. I shuddered as the darkest corner of the attic beckoned me to come explore.
    b. Your gum chewing sounds like cows walking through mud.
    c. How did you get that purple-green golf ball–sized lump above your eye?

Name _____

PART II

Below are eight different writing tasks. For each one, follow the directions given at the beginning of the task. Each task is worth 10 points.

TASK 1 Each underlined word is an overused word or phrase. Replace each one with something more interesting and fresh—a word or phrase that is more effective or appealing to the reader.

This is a tale of <u>trouble</u>—unhappy, <u>big</u> <u>trouble</u>. It began when I <u>walked</u> into a dark corner behind the old shed. Right away, I knew I should have <u>moved out</u> of there <u>quicker than a wink</u>.

TASK 2 Rearrange the words in these sentences to make the sentences more clear.

1. Scott whistled to his dog driving his motorcycle. _____
   _____

2. Riding a bike in the morning, the sun was getting hot on my back. _____
   _____

3. My sister liked to tell her favorite jokes when we had the preacher's family for dinner. _____
   _____

TASK 3 Write a sentence that has interesting sounds and rhythms. Use some of these words, if you'd like to. You can add others, or you can use all your own words.

flitter	thrice	bubbles	gadzooks
flutter	African	buggy	mush
cruise	generation	gopher	shush
news	obligation	loafer	hush
bruise	conflagration	information	sloshes
ounce	mitigation	kooks	galoshes
dice	boggle	nukes	

_____
_____
_____

TASK 4 Remove the excess words in these sentences by crossing them out.

1. There were these three kids who were friends who came up with a plan to totally eat a whole cow.
2. Abby made a geometric design in math class that had four shapes that were squares, seven three-sided triangles, and six round circles.

TASK 5 Use these short sentences to form a short paragraph. Combine the sentences in interesting ways so that you create a paragraph which has variety in sentence length and structure.

It started suddenly.
Before we knew it, things were out of control.
Tom sneezed.
Matt fell backwards.
Matt knocked Jon over.
Jon's bike fell.
His bike crashed into Dave's horse.
The horse bolted.
The garage door was in the way.
Were we in trouble!

_____
_____
_____
_____

TASK 6 Write a strong beginning for one of these sample topics.

An accident
A visit from a very strange stranger
An unplanned trip into the past
An unplanned trip into the future
Being in the wrong place at the wrong time
The test you forgot about
A topic of your choice

_____
_____
_____
_____

Name _____

TASK 7 Write a strong ending for one of these sample topics.

The most embarrassing moment of your life
A locked place
The trouble you may or may not have gotten out of
A person you wish you'd never met
A place you're glad you went
A place you never wanted to go
A piece of information you stumbled across
A topic of your choice

_____

_____

_____

_____

_____

_____

_____

_____

_____

_____

_____

_____

_____

_____

_____

_____

_____

TASK 8 Rewrite this brief story using dialogue.

She ran to the police station and tried to explain that the car had gone into the bakery through the window. She said that several people on the sidewalk hollered at the driver to stop, but it didn't help. She told the police sergeant that the bakers were screaming for help and that there were pastries and frosting everywhere and people grabbing baked goods. She also told him that kids were cheering and saying that free doughnuts were rolling down the street. She insisted that there was chaos and that someone needed to come quickly. The policeman responded by asking if she would please state her name, address, and social security number.

_____

_____

_____

_____

_____

_____

_____

_____

_____

_____

_____

_____

_____

_____

_____

SCORE: Total Points _____ out of a possible 100 points

Name

_____

WRITING
SKILLS TEST ANSWER KEY

Part I

Students may choose answers for questions 1–20 that vary slightly from the answers given below, as word choices and sentence interpretation are subjective acts. Give student credit for any reasonable answer.

1. c
2. a
3. b
4. a
5. d
6. b
7. c
8. d
9. b
10. b, c
11. a, c
12. a, b
13. a, b
14. a
15. a
16. (answers will vary): old, who was kind of like, together
17. a
18. a, b, c
19. b
20. b

PART II

Answers will vary considerably on these eight writing tasks. There are no right and wrong answers. Give students up to 10 points for each task, judged on:

a) how thoroughly they completed the task
b) if they followed the directions
c) if they succeeded in accomplishing what was asked of them

ANSWERS

For most of the activities in these pages, the answers will vary. Check to see that students have completed the tasks with reasonable responses that fit the requirements of the tasks, that they have taken the directions seriously, and that they have given effort to completing the exercise as explained. Answers are listed below for the pages that have specific answers.

page 13

Answers may vary somewhat.
1. OK
2. The bad joke embarrassed us.
3. Someone stole my purse.
4. OK
5. They put the thief in jail. OR, The thief went to jail.
6. OK
7. Have you recorded the grades?
8. No one has ever told the story.
9. Did the Easter Bunny bring those eggs?
10. Did an elephant sit on this hat?

page 16

Answers may vary somewhat.
1. The reason she refused his invitation to the dance was that she had nothing to wear.
2. We couldn't hear the words to the song because the track was too loud.
3. The room was square.
4. If students cooperate, they can outwit the teacher.
5. John's attitude was bad.
6. In my opinion, the assignment is unfair. Or, I think the assignment is unfair.
7. He drew three circles on his paper.
8. I think the bald principal is kind of cute.
9. Chad is a great player. Or, Chad really plays well.
10. I would like a new friend.
11. My parents monitor everything I do.
12. Waitress, what is today's soup?

page 18

Answers will vary somewhat. These are some possibilities.
1. While I was cleaning the attic this morning, a mouse scared me.
2. As we were paddling quietly along in the canoe, the moon shone brightly.
3. In the morning paper, I read about the bank robbers who were caught.
4. The students were worried that the teacher, having collapsed in a convulsion of laughter, would never regain consciousness.
5. So that Joey could earn money for the prom, Mr. Blake gave him a job mowing his lawn.
6. The fans in the stands booed the football players.
7. While Fluffy was eating her cat food, Mom noticed that she had a burr in her paw.
8. When I was a child, my mother taught me many lessons.
9. Behind the junkyard, there was a tiny cottage that was very beautiful.
10. I could not find my math book on the top shelf of my locker.
11. He sold ice cream sodas with tiny umbrellas in them to the children.
12. The eighth graders were punished by the principal after the fire alarm prank.

page 21

"Gotcha!": The victim is a mosquito.

page 22

The housekeeper could not open the mailbox because the key was in the box since he sent it through the mail.

page 32

Answers will vary slightly.
Some possible answers:
1. formal, defensive, accusatory, imploring
2. leisurely, languid, relaxed, free
3. dark, foreboding, ominous